100 facts

WEATHER

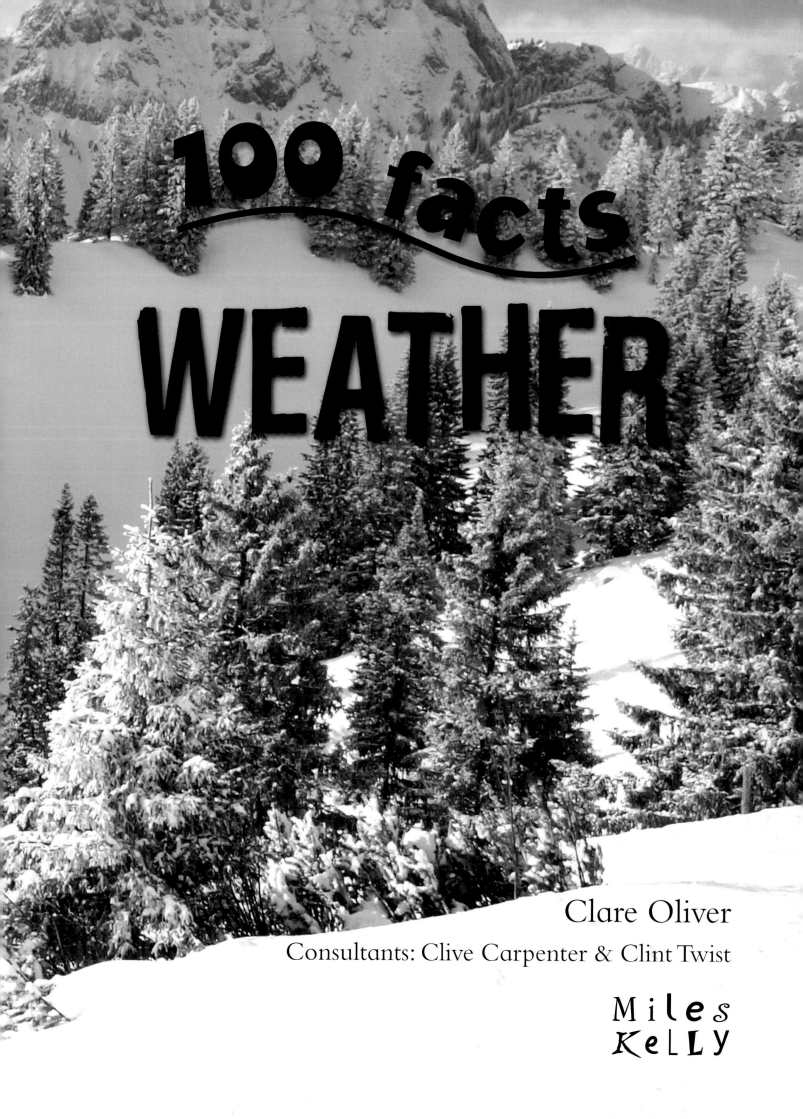

100 facts

WEATHER

Clare Oliver

Consultants: Clive Carpenter & Clint Twist

Miles Kelly

First published in 2002 by Miles Kelly Publishing Ltd
Harding's Barn, Bardfield End Green, Thaxted, Essex, CM6 3PX, UK

Copyright © Miles Kelly Publishing 2002

This updated edition printed in 2014

6 8 10 9 7

Publishing Director Belinda Gallagher
Creative Director Jo Cowan
Editorial Director Rosie Neave
Assistant Editor Amy Johnson
Designers Rob Hale, Venita Kidwai, John Christopher (White Design)
Production Manager Elizabeth Collins
Reprographics Stephan Davis, Jennifer Hunt, Thom Allaway
Assets Lorraine King

ISBN 978-1-78209-076-2

Printed in China

British Library Cataloguing-in-Publication Data
A catalogue record for this book is available from the British Library

ACKNOWLEDGEMENTS

The publishers would like to thank Sylvia Knight for her help in updating this book.

The publishers would like to thank the following sources for the use of their photographs:
Key: t = top, b = bottom, c = centre, l = left, r = right, m = main

Cover (front) Creative Travel Projects/Shutterstock, (back, t) Andrzej Gibasiewicz/Shutterstock
Corbis 15 Robert Holmes; 42(l) Michele Eve Sandberg; 44–45 Jim Reed/Science Faction **Dreamstime** 5(tr) and 33(c); 29(t) Wickedgood;
33(b) Astrofireball; 47(b) Naluphoto **FLPA** 17(b) Yva Momatiuk & John Eastcott/Minden Pictures
Fotolia paper (throughout) Sharpshot; 8(b) Sharpshot **iStock** 5(b) Tobias Helbig; 6(bl) David Mathies; 9(t) alohaspirit; 33(t) Scene_It;
34(m) Sean Randall; 47(t) luoman **NASA** 5(tl) and 44(t) NASA/Lori Losey; 14(bl) NASA/JPL/UCSD/JSC; 45(tl) Jesse Allen, Earth
Observatory **Rex** 21(m); KeystoneUSA-ZUMA **Shutterstock** 1 behindlens; 2–3 and 6(tl) Seriousjoy, (c) Kevin Eaves, (br) Asaf Eliason;
7(tl) haveseen, (tr) Wild Arctic Pictures, (c) Pichugin Dmitry, (br) Oleg Znamenskiy, (bl) Tatiana Popova; 8(t) Redsapphire; 10(m) 1000
Words, (tr) Morozova Oxana, (b) Mark Sayer; 11(b) Dmitriy Bryndin; 12–13(m) Roca; 13(t) Loskutnikov; 16(b) Alexandr Zyryanov;
19(b) Christy Nicholas; 20(t) Olivier Le Queinec, (m) Mike Buchheit; 22(m) Bull's-Eye Arts; 23(tl) Brandelet, (tr) Mikhail Pogosov,
(b) Armin Rose; 24(t) @cam; 25(bl) Stephen Meese, (Force 0) Tudor Spinu, (Force 1) Sinelyov, (Force 2) Jennifer Griner, (Force 4) Vlue,
(Force 5) Martin Preston, (Force 6) behindlens, (Force 7) photobank.kiev.ua, (Force 8) Robert Hoetink, (Force 9) Slobodan Djajic,
(Force 10) Ortodox, (Force 11) Dustie, (Force 12) Melissa Brandes; 26–27 kornilov007; 27(bl) Sam DCruz, (c) Gunnar Pippel,
(tl) Jack Dagley Photography; 31(bl) DarkOne, (br) javarman; 32(m) PhotoHouse, (bl) pzAxe; 34(t) EcoPrint; 35(t) outdoorsman,
(b) Jean-Edouard Rozey; 37(l) Patryk Kosmider, (r) riekephotos; 38(m) AdamEdwards; 39(t) photomaster, (b) Squarciomomo;
40(t) Khirman Vladimir; 40–41(b) Steve Mann; 41(c) AISPIX by Image Source; 43(b) Map Resources; 45(r) George Burba;
46(m) Lee Prince **SPL** 16–17(m) Gary Hincks **Wikimedia commons** 13(c) Arthur Rothstein; 41(b) Olof Arenius

All other photographs are from:
digitalSTOCK, digitalvision, ImageState,
John Foxx, PhotoAlto, PhotoDisc, PhotoEssentials, PhotoPro, Stockbyte

All artworks are from the Miles Kelly Artwork Bank

Every effort has been made to acknowledge the source and copyright holder of each picture.
Miles Kelly Publishing apologizes for any unintentional errors or omissions.

Made with paper from a sustainable forest

www.mileskelly.net
info@mileskelly.net

Contents

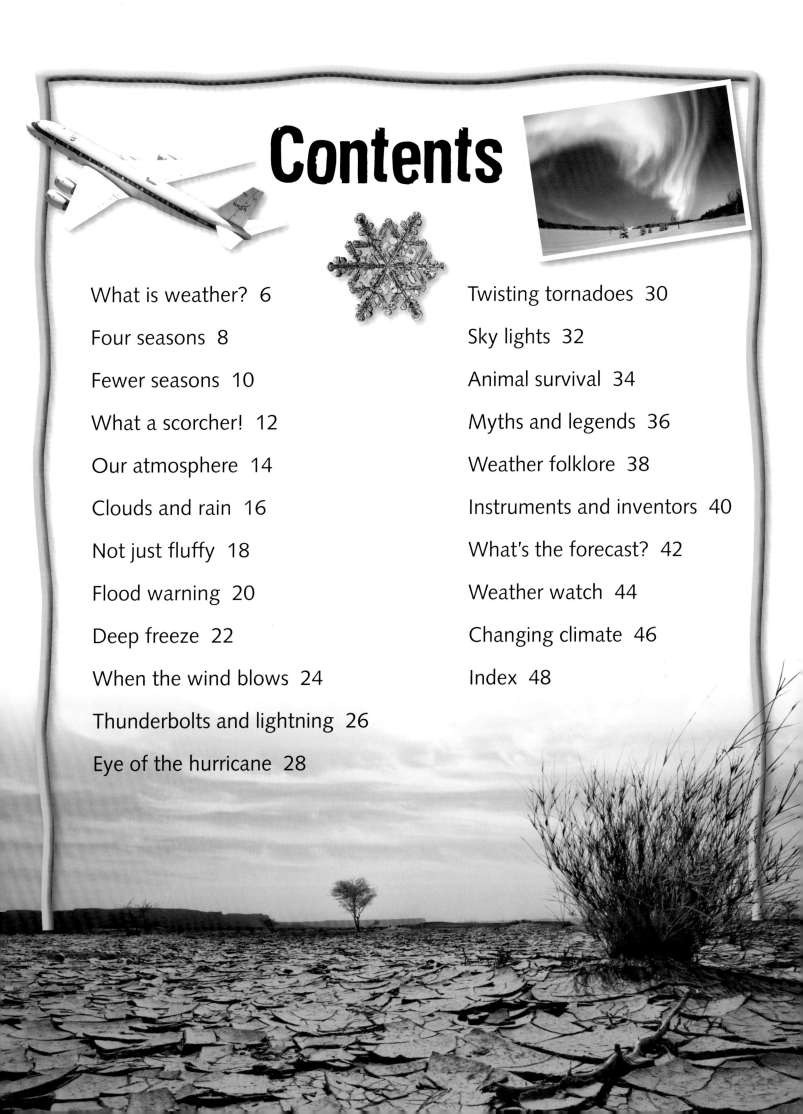

What is weather?

1 Rain, sunshine, snow and storms are all types of weather. Different weather is caused by what is happening in the atmosphere – the air around us and above our heads. In some parts of the world, the weather changes every day, but in others, it is nearly always the same. Weather affects how animals, plants and people survive and behave.

▼ This map shows the different types of climate that are found in different places around the world.

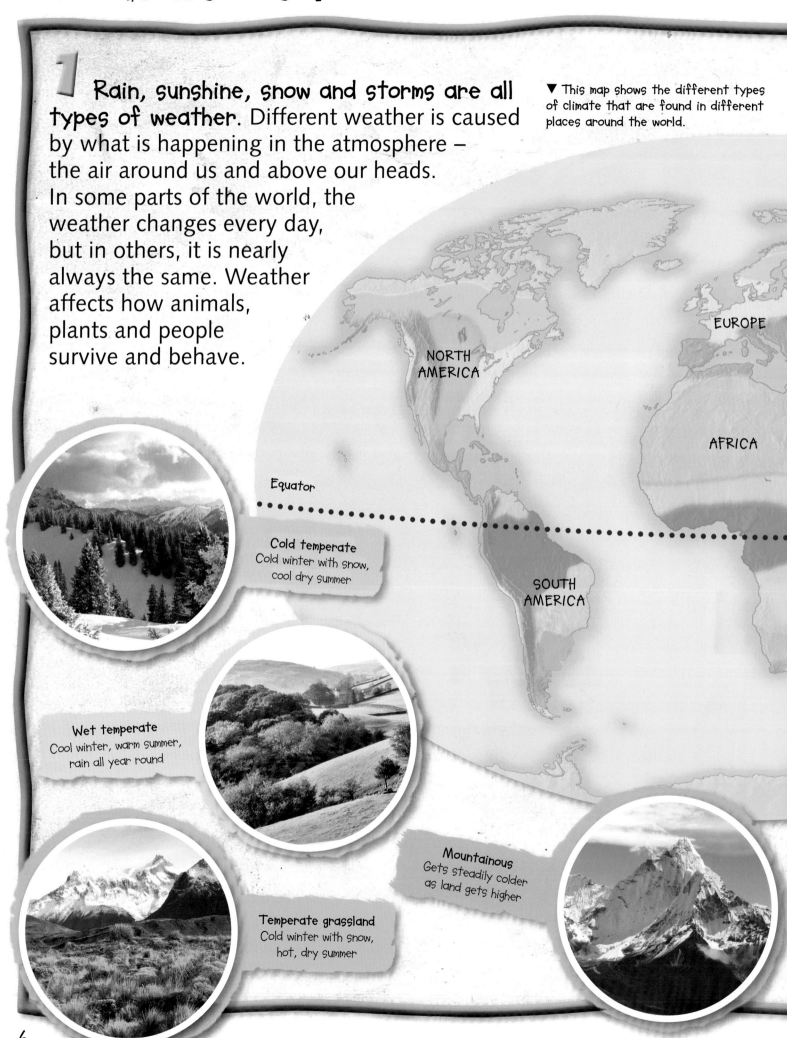

NORTH AMERICA

EUROPE

AFRICA

Equator

SOUTH AMERICA

Cold temperate
Cold winter with snow, cool dry summer

Wet temperate
Cool winter, warm summer, rain all year round

Temperate grassland
Cold winter with snow, hot, dry summer

Mountainous
Gets steadily colder as land gets higher

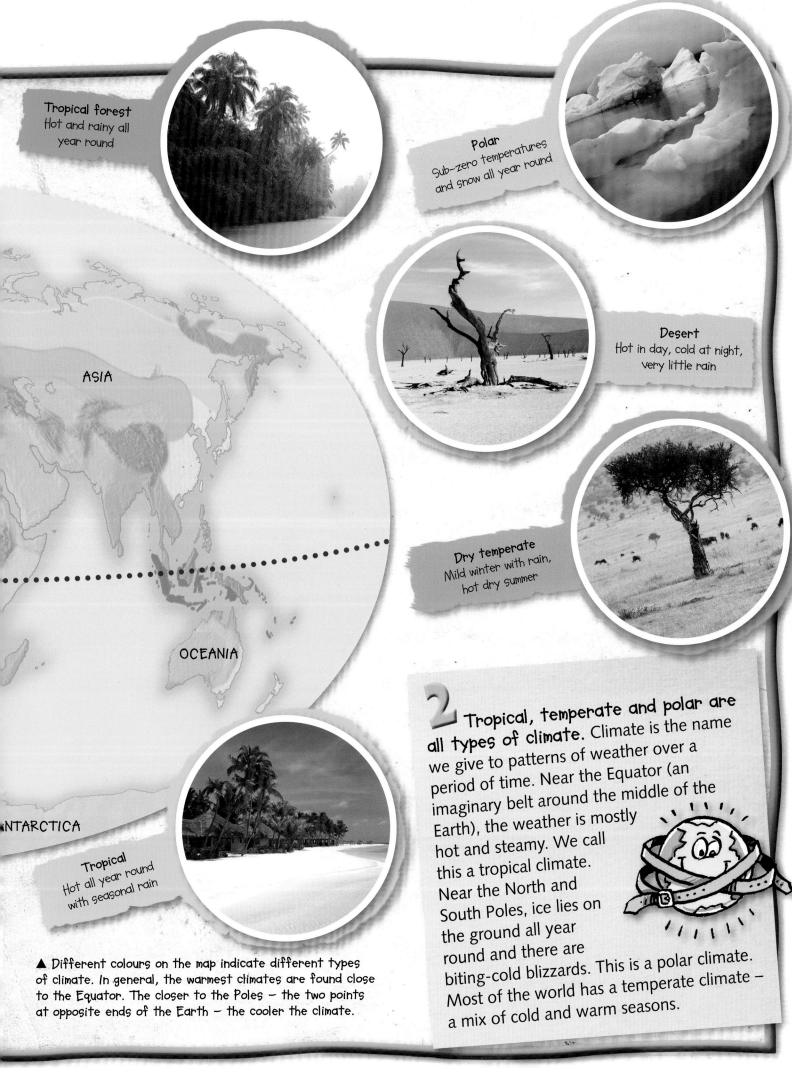

Tropical forest
Hot and rainy all
year round

Polar
Sub–zero temperatures
and snow all year round

Desert
Hot in day, cold at night,
very little rain

ASIA

Dry temperate
Mild winter with rain,
hot dry summer

OCEANIA

ANTARCTICA

Tropical
Hot all year round
with seasonal rain

▲ Different colours on the map indicate different types
of climate. In general, the warmest climates are found close
to the Equator. The closer to the Poles — the two points
at opposite ends of the Earth — the cooler the climate.

2 **Tropical, temperate and polar are
all types of climate.** Climate is the name
we give to patterns of weather over a
period of time. Near the Equator (an
imaginary belt around the middle of the
Earth), the weather is mostly
hot and steamy. We call
this a tropical climate.
Near the North and
South Poles, ice lies on
the ground all year
round and there are
biting-cold blizzards. This is a polar climate.
Most of the world has a temperate climate —
a mix of cold and warm seasons.

Four seasons

3 **The reason we have seasons lies in space.** Due to the pull of the Sun's gravity, Earth is on a continuous path through space that takes it around the Sun. This path, or orbit, takes one year. The Earth is tilted, so over the year first one and then the other Pole leans towards the Sun, giving us seasons. In June, for example, the North Pole is tilted towards the Sun. The Sun heats the northern half of the Earth and it is summer.

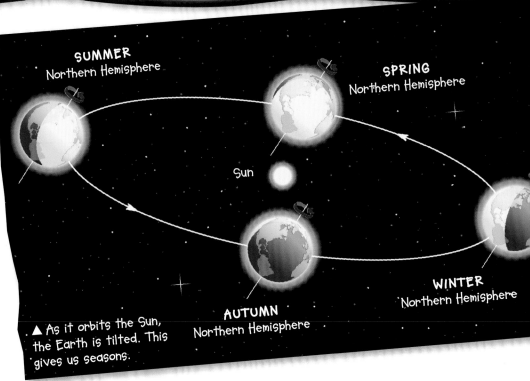

SUMMER
Northern Hemisphere

SPRING
Northern Hemisphere

Sun

AUTUMN
Northern Hemisphere

WINTER
Northern Hemisphere

▲ As it orbits the Sun, the Earth is tilted. This gives us seasons.

4 **When it is summer in Argentina, it is winter in Canada.** In December, the South Pole leans towards the Sun. Places in the southern half of the world, such as Argentina, have summer. At the same time, places in the northern half, such as Canada, have winter.

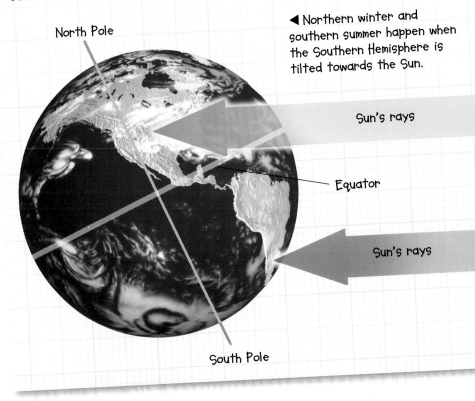

North Pole

◄ Northern winter and southern summer happen when the Southern Hemisphere is tilted towards the Sun.

Sun's rays

Equator

Sun's rays

South Pole

I DON'T BELIEVE IT!

When the Sun shines all day in the far north, there is 24-hour night in the far south.

▼ Near the North Pole, the Sun never sets below the horizon on Midsummer's Day.

5 **A day can last 21 hours!** Night and day happen because Earth is spinning as it circles the Sun. At the height of summer, places near the North Pole are so tilted towards the Sun that it is light almost all day long. In Stockholm, Sweden on Midsummer's Eve, daytime lasts for 21 hours because the Sun disappears below the horizon for only three hours.

▶ Trees that lose their leaves in autumn are called deciduous. Evergreens are trees that keep their leaves all year round.

AUTUMN

Leaves change colour and start to fall. Fruits ripen.

WINTER

Branches are bare.

SUMMER

Flowering trees are in full bloom. Some have a second growth spurt.

SPRING

Leaf buds start to grow. The leaves soon open and flowers bloom.

6 **Some forests change colour in the autumn.** Autumn comes between summer and winter. Trees prepare for the cold winter months ahead by losing their leaves. First, though, they suck back the precious green chlorophyll, or dye, in their leaves, making them turn glorious shades of red, orange and brown.

Fewer seasons

7 Monsoons are winds that carry heavy rains. The rains fall in the tropics in summer during the hot, rainy season. The Sun warms up the sea, which causes huge banks of cloud to form. Monsoons then blow these clouds towards land. Once the rains hit the continent, they can pour for weeks.

▲ When monsoon rains are especially heavy, they can cause chaos. Streets turn to rivers and sometimes people's homes are washed away.

8 Monsoons happen mainly in Asia. However, there are parts of the Americas, close to the Equator, that also have a rainy season. Winds can carry heavy rain clouds, causing flash floods in the southwestern deserts of the USA. The floods happen because the land has been baked hard during the dry season so water doesn't drain away.

POTENTIAL FLASH FLOOD AREAS

NEXT 6 MILES

◄ This sign warns of flash flooding in California, USA.

9 **Many parts of the tropics have two seasons, not four.** They are the parts of the world closest to the Equator. Here it is always hot, as these places are constantly facing the Sun. However, the Earth's movement affects the position of a great band of cloud. In June, the tropical areas north of the Equator have the strongest heat and the heaviest rainstorms. In December, it is the turn of the areas south of the Equator.

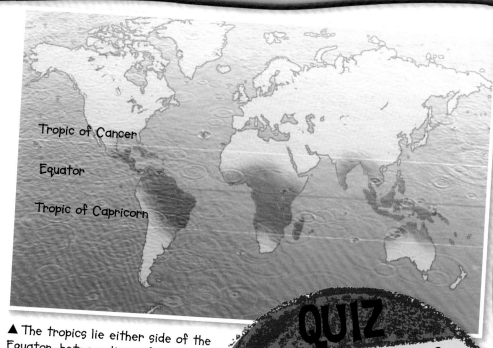

Tropic of Cancer

Equator

Tropic of Capricorn

▲ The tropics lie either side of the Equator, between lines of latitude called the Tropic of Cancer and the Tropic of Capricorn.

QUIZ

1. What are monsoons?
2. On which continent do most monsoons occur?
3. How many seasons are there in the tropics?
4. How much rainfall do tropical rainforests usually have in a year?

Answers:
1. Winds that carry heavy rains 2. Asia 3. Two 4. About 2000 millimetres

◀ Daily rainfall feeds lush rainforest vegetation and countless waterfalls in the mountains of Costa Rica.

10 **Tropical rainforests have rainy weather all year round.** There is usually about 2000 millimetres of rainfall in a year. Rainforests still have a wet and a dry season, but the wet season is even wetter! Some parts of the rainforest can become flooded during the wet season, as the heavy rain makes rivers overflow their banks.

What a scorcher!

QUIZ

1. Where is the hottest recorded place in the world?
2. When did the 'Dust Bowl' occur?
3. What caused the 'Dust Bowl'?
4. Is El Niño a wind or a current?

Answers:
1. Death Valley in California, USA 2. The 1930s 3. Terrible drought 4. A current

11 All of our heat comes from the Sun. The Sun is a star, a super-hot ball of burning gases. It gives off heat rays that travel 150 million kilometres through space to reach Earth. During the journey, the rays cool down, but they are still hot enough to scorch the Earth.

12 The Sahara is the sunniest place on Earth. This North African desert once had 4300 hours of sunshine in a year! People who live here, such as the Tuareg Arabs, cover their skin to avoid being sunburnt.

► Desert peoples wear headdresses to protect their skin and eyes from the sun and sand.

13 The hottest temperature on Earth was measured at Death Valley in California, USA. An air temperature of 56.7°C was recorded in 1913. Al Aziziyah in Libya had held a record of 58°C for 90 years, but in 2012 this was reanalyzed and found to be incorrect.

14 **The Sun can trick your eyes.** Sometimes, as sunlight passes through our atmosphere, it hits layers of air at different temperatures. When this happens, the air bends the light and can trick our eyes into seeing something that is not there. This is a mirage. For example, what looks like a pool of water might really be part of the sky reflected on to the land.

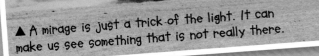

▲ A mirage is just a trick of the light. It can make us see something that is not really there.

15 **Too much sun brings drought.** Clear skies and sunshine are not always good news. Without rain, crops wither, and people and their animals go hungry.

16 **One terrible drought made a 'Dust Bowl'.** Settlements in the American Midwest were devestated by a long drought during the 1930s. As crops died, there were no roots to hold the soil together. The dry earth turned to dust and some farms simply blew away!

▼ During the 1930s, dust storms caused by drought in Oklahoma, USA covered fields in layers of dust.

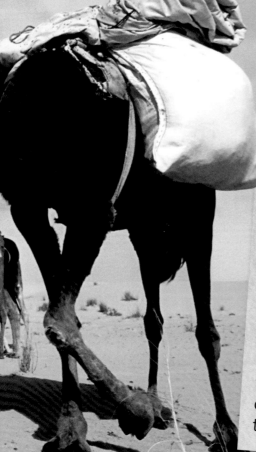

Warm water

OCEANIA

PACIFIC OCEAN

SOUTH AMERICA

Cold water

▲ El Niño has been known to cause violent weather conditions. It returns on average every four years.

17 **A sea current can set forests alight.** All sorts of things affect our weather and climate. The movements of a sea current called El Niño have been blamed for causing flooding and terrible droughts – which can lead to unstoppable forest fires.

Our atmosphere

18 **Our planet is wrapped in a blanket of air.** We call this blanket the atmosphere. It stretches hundreds of kilometres above our heads. The atmosphere keeps in heat, especially at night when part of the planet faces away from the Sun. During the day, it becomes a sunscreen instead, protecting us from the Sun's fierce rays. Without an atmosphere, there would be no weather.

19 **Most weather happens in the troposphere.** This is the layer of atmosphere that stretches from the ground to around 10 kilometres above your head. The higher in the troposphere you go, the cooler the air. Because of this, clouds are most likely to form here. Clouds with flattened tops show just where the troposphere meets the next layer, the stratosphere.

KEY

1. Exosphere
   190 to 960 kilometres
2. Thermosphere
   80 to 190 kilometres
3. Mesosphere
   50 to 80 kilometres
4. Stratosphere
   10 to 50 kilometres
5. Troposphere
   0 to 10 kilometres

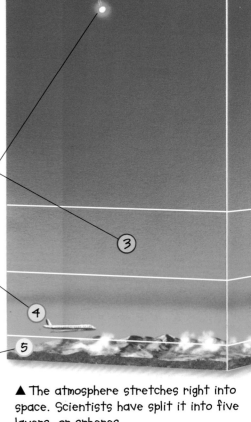

Low-level satellites orbit within the exosphere

The Northern and Southern Lights – the auroras – are formed in the thermosphere

Meteors entering the amosphere burn up in the mesosphere, causing 'shooting stars'

Aeroplanes either fly high in the troposphere, or in the lower levels of the stratosphere

Weather forms in the troposphere

▶ This view of the Earth from the International Space Station, which orbits the Earth, shows the atmosphere as a thin, wispy layer.

▲ The atmosphere stretches right into space. Scientists have split it into five layers, or spheres.

20 Air just cannot keep still. Tiny particles in air, called molecules, are always bumping into each other. The more they do this, the greater the air pressure. Generally, there are more collisions lower in the troposphere, because the pull of gravity makes the molecules fall towards the Earth's surface. The higher you go, the lower the air pressure, and the less oxygen there is in the air.

21 Warmth makes air move. When heat from the Sun warms the molecules in air, they move faster and spread out more. This makes the air lighter, so it rises in the sky, creating low pressure. As it gets higher, the air cools. The molecules slow down and become heavier again, so they start to sink back to Earth.

HIGH PRESSURE

LOW PRESSURE

Cool air sinking

Warm air rising

Centre of high pressure

Air flow moves in clockwise direction

Centre of low pressure

Air flow moves in anticlockwise direction

▲ A high pressure weather system gives us warmer weather, while low pressure gives us cooler, more unsettled weather. (In the Northern Hemisphere, air flows anticlockwise in a low pressure system, and clockwise in high pressure. In the Southern Hemisphere, it is the opposite.)

▲ At high altitudes there is less oxygen. That is why mountaineers often wear breathing equipment.

Clouds and rain

22 **Rain comes from the sea.** As the Sun heats the surface of the ocean, some seawater turns into water vapour and rises into the air. As it rises, it cools and turns back into water droplets. Lots of water droplets make clouds. The droplets join together to make bigger and bigger drops that eventually fall as rain. Some rain is soaked up by the land, but a lot finds its way back to the sea. This is called the water cycle.

23 **Some mountains are so tall that their summits (peaks) are hidden by cloud.** They can even affect the weather. When moving air hits a mountain slope it is forced upwards. As it travels up, the temperature drops, and clouds form.

▼ The peak of Chapaeva, in the Tian Shan mountain range in Asia, can be seen above the clouds.

KEY	
1	Water evaporates from the sea
2	Clouds form
3	Water is given off by trees
4	Rain falls, filling rivers
5	Rivers run back to the sea

WARM AIR

▼ Water moves in a continuous cycle between the ocean, atmosphere and land.

24 **Clouds release energy.** When water vapour becomes water droplets and forms clouds, a small amount of heat energy is given out into the atmosphere. Then, when the droplets fall as rain, kinetic, or movement, energy is released as the rain hits the ground.

RAIN GAUGE

You will need:
jam jar   waterproof marker pen
ruler   notebook   pen

Put the jar outside. At the same time each day, mark the rainwater level on the jar with your pen. At the end of a week, empty the jar. Measure and record how much rain fell each day and over the whole week.

▶ Virga happens when rain reaches a layer of dry air. The rain droplets turn back into water vapour in mid-air, and seem to disappear.

25 **Some rain never reaches the ground.** The raindrops turn back into water vapour because they hit a layer of super-dry air. You can actually see the drops falling like a curtain from the cloud, but the curtain stops in mid-air. This type of weather is called virga.

Not just fluffy

26 Clouds come in all shapes and sizes. Scientists divide clouds into three basic types – cirrus, stratus, and cumulus – according to their shape and height above the ground. Cirrus clouds look like wisps of smoke. They form high in the troposphere and rarely mean rain. Stratus clouds form in flat layers and may produce drizzle or a sprinkling of snow. Most types of cumulus clouds bring rain. They look soft and fluffy.

27 Not all cumulus clouds produce rain. Cumulus humilis clouds are the smallest heap-shaped clouds. In the sky, they look like lumpy, cotton wool sausages! They are too small to produce rain but they can grow into much bigger, rain-carrying cumulus clouds. The biggest cumulus clouds, called cumulonimbus, bring heavy rainfall.

Cirrus
Thin, wispy high-level clouds, sometimes called 'mare's tails'

Cumulonimbus
Towering grey-white clouds that produce heavy rainfall

Cumulus
Billowing clouds with flat bases

Nimbostratus
Dense layer of low, grey rain clouds

▶ The main classes of cloud – cirrus, cumulus and stratus – were named in the 1800s. An amateur British weather scientist called Luke Howard identified the different types.

Cirrocumulus
Ripples or rows of small white clouds at high altitude

Contrails
The white streaks created by planes

Altocumulus
Small globular clouds at middle altitude

28 Not all clouds are made by nature. Contrails are streaky clouds that a plane leaves behind it as it flies. They are made of water vapour that comes from the plane's engines. The second it hits the cold air, the vapour turns into ice crystals, leaving a trail of white cloud.

Altostratus
Layered grey middle-level cloud with no visible holes

29 Sometimes the sky is filled with white patches of cloud that look like shimmering fish scales. These are called mackerel skies. It takes lots of gusty wind to break the cloud into these little patches, and so mackerel skies are usually a sign of changeable weather.

Stratocumulus
Grey clouds in patches or globules that may join together

◄ A mackerel sky over Calanais stone circle in Scotland.

Stratus
Continuous low cloud near, but not touching, the ground

Flood warning

▲ The power of flood water has caused great damage to this house in Australia.

30 **Too much rain brings flooding.** There are two different types of floods. Flash floods happen after a short burst of heavy rainfall, usually caused by thunderstorms. Broadscale flooding happens when rain falls steadily over a wide area – for weeks or months – without stopping. When this happens, rivers slowly fill and eventually burst their banks. Tropical storms, such as hurricanes, can also lead to broadscale flooding.

31 **There can be floods in the desert.** When a lot of rain falls very quickly on to land that has been baked dry, it cannot soak in. Instead, it sits on the surface, causing flash floods.

▼ A desert flash flood in the Grand Canyon, USA, has created streams of muddy water. After the water level falls, vegetation will burst into life.

I DON'T BELIEVE IT!

The ancient Egyptians had a story to explain the yearly flooding of the Nile. They said the goddess Isis filled the river with tears, as she cried for her lost husband.

32 There really was a
Great Flood. The Bible tells of a
terrible flood, and how a man called
Noah was saved. Recently, explorers
found the first real evidence of the
flood – a sunken beach 140 metres
below the surface of the Black Sea.
There are ruins of houses, dating
back to 5600 BC. Stories of a flood
in ancient times do not only appear
in the Bible – the Babylonians and
Greeks told of one, too.

▼ In the Bible, Noah
survived the Great
Flood by building a
huge wooden
boat called
an ark.

33 Mud can flood.
When rain mixes with earth
it makes mud. On bare
mountainsides, there are no tree
roots to hold the soil together.
An avalanche of mud can slide
off the mountain. The worst
ever mudslide happened after
flooding in Colombia,
South America in 1985. It
buried 23,000 people from the
town of Armero.

◀ Torrential rain in Brazil caused
this mudslide, which swept away
part of a village.

21

Deep freeze

▶ This truck has become stuck in a snow drift. Falling snow is made worse by strong winds, which can form deep drifts.

34 Snow is made of tiny ice crystals. When air temperatures are very cold – around 0°C – the water droplets in the clouds freeze to make tiny ice crystals. Sometimes, individual crystals fall, but usually they clump together into snowflakes.

35 No two snowflakes are the same. This is because snowflakes are made up of ice crystals, and every ice crystal is as unique as your fingerprint. Most crystals look like six-pointed stars, but they come in other shapes too.

▼ A snowflake that is several centimetres across will be made up of lots of crystals, like these.

36 Black ice is not really black. Drizzle or rain turns to ice when it touches freezing-cold ground. This 'black' ice is see-through, and hard to spot against a road's dark tarmac. It is also very slippery, creating dangerous driving conditions.

I DON'T BELIEVE IT!
Antarctica is the coldest place on Earth. Temperatures of −89.2°C have been recorded there.

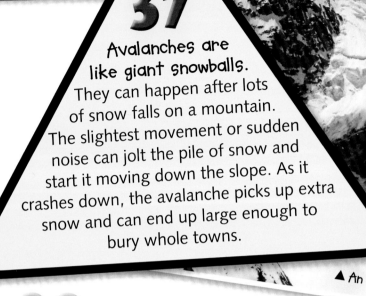

37

Avalanches are like giant snowballs. They can happen after lots of snow falls on a mountain. The slightest movement or sudden noise can jolt the pile of snow and start it moving down the slope. As it crashes down, the avalanche picks up extra snow and can end up large enough to bury whole towns.

▲ An avalanche gathers speed as it thunders down the mountainside.

38

Marksmen shoot at snowy mountains. One way to prevent deadly avalanches is to stop too much snow from building up. In mountainous areas, marksmen set off mini avalanches on purpose. They make sure people are out of the danger zone, then fire guns to trigger a snowslide.

▼ Antarctica is a frozen wilderness. The ice piles up to form amazing shapes.

39

Ice can stay frozen for millions of years. At the North and South Poles, the weather never warms up enough for the ice to thaw. When fresh snow falls, it presses down on the snow already there, forming thick sheets. Some ice may not have melted for a million years or more.

When the wind blows

40 **Wind is moving air.** The wind blows because air is constantly moving from areas of high pressure to areas of low pressure. The bigger the difference in pressure between the two areas, the faster the wind blows.

▶ In open, exposed areas, trees can be forced into strange shapes by the wind.

41 **Winds have names.** World wind patterns are called global winds. The most famous are the trade winds that blow towards the Equator. There are also well-known local winds, such as the cold, dry mistral that blows down to southern France, or the hot, dry sirroco that blows north of the Sahara.

▼ This map shows the pattern of the world's main winds.

North Pole
Polar easterlies
Westerlies
Equator
Trade winds
Westerlies
Polar easterlies
South Pole

42 **Trade winds blow from east to west, above and below the Equator.** In the tropics, air is moving to an area of low pressure at the Equator. The winds blow towards the Equator, from the southeast in the Southern Hemisphere, and the northeast in the Northern Hemisphere. Their name comes from their importance to traders, when goods travelled across the oceans by sailing ship.

43 You can tell how windy it is by looking at the leaves on a tree. Wind strength is measured on the Beaufort Scale, named after the Irish admiral who devised it. The scale is based on the visible effects of wind, and ranges from Force 0, meaning total calm, to Force 12, which is a hurricane.

44 Wind can bring very changeable weather. The Föhn wind, which blows across Switzerland, Austria and Bavaria in southern Germany, brings with it significant and rapid rises in temperature, sometimes by as much as 30°C in a matter of hours. This has been blamed for various illnesses, including bouts of madness!

45 Wind can turn on your TV. People can harness the energy of wind to make electricity for our homes. Tall turbines are positioned in windy places. As the wind turns the turbine, the movement powers a generator and produces electrical energy.

▼ Wind energy doesn't create any harmful pollution, and it will never run out.

The Beaufort Scale

Force 0: Calm
Smoke rises straight up

Force 1: Light air
Wind motion visible in smoke

Force 2: Light breeze
Leaves rustle

Force 3: Gentle breeze
Twigs move, light flags flap

Force 4: Moderate breeze
Small branches move

Force 5: Fresh breeze
Bushes and small trees sway

Force 6: Strong breeze
Large branches in motion

Force 7: Near gale
Whole trees sway

Force 8: Gale
Difficult to walk or move, twigs break

Force 9: Strong gale
Tiles and chimneys may be blown from rooftops

Force 10: Storm
Trees uprooted

Force 11: Violent storm
Widespread damage to buildings

Force 12: Hurricane
Severe devastation

Thunderbolts and lightning

46 **Thunderstorms are most likely to occur in summer.** Hot weather creates warm, moist air that rises and forms towering cumulonimbus clouds. Inside each cloud, water droplets and ice crystals move about, building up positive and negative electrical charges. Electricity flows between the charges, creating a flash that heats the air around it. Lightning is so hot that it makes the air expand, making a loud noise, or thunderclap.

▼ Cloud-to-cloud lightning is called sheet lightning. Lightning travelling from the cloud to the ground, as shown here, is called fork lightning.

HOW CLOSE?

Lightning and thunder happen at the same time, but light travels faster than sound. Count the seconds between the flash and the clap and divide them by three. This is how many kilometres away the storm is.

▼ Dramatic lightning flashes in Arizona, USA, light up the sky.

47 **Lightning comes in different colours.** If there is rain in the thundercloud, the lightning looks red or pink, and if there's hail, it looks blue. Lightning can also be yellow or white.

▼ Hailstones can be huge! These ones are as big as a golf ball.

48 Chunks of ice called hailstones can fall from thunderclouds. The biggest hailstones fell in Gopaljang, Bangladesh, in 1986 and weighed one kilogram each!

49 A person can survive a lightning strike. Lightning is very dangerous and can give a big enough electric shock to kill you. However, an American park ranger called Roy Sullivan survived being struck seven times.

50 Tall buildings are protected from lightning. Church steeples and other tall structures are often struck by bolts of lightning. This could damage the building, or give electric shocks to people inside, so lightning conductors are placed on the roof. These channel the lightning safely away.

◄ If lightning hits a conductor it is carried safely to the ground.

Eye of the hurricane

51 Some winds travel at speeds of more than 120 kilometres an hour. Violent tropical storms such as hurricanes happen when strong winds blow into an area of low pressure and start spinning very fast. They develop over warm seas and pick up speed until they reach land, where there is no more moist sea air to feed them.

52 The centre of a hurricane is calm and still. This part is called the 'eye'. As the eye of the storm passes over, there is a pause in the terrifying rain and wind.

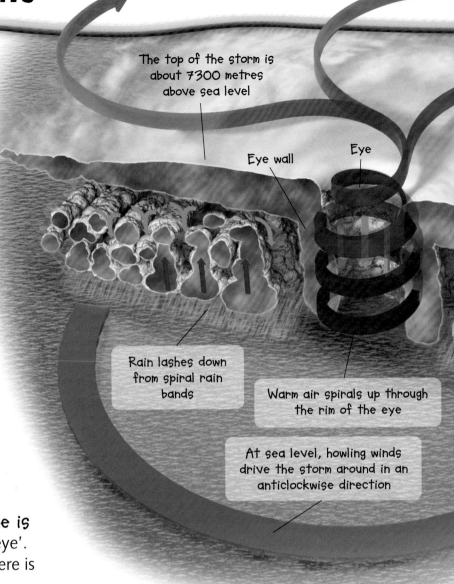

The top of the storm is about 7300 metres above sea level

Eye wall

Eye

Rain lashes down from spiral rain bands

Warm air spirals up through the rim of the eye

At sea level, howling winds drive the storm around in an anticlockwise direction

▲ This satellite photograph shows how the storm whirls around the central, still 'eye' of the hurricane.

53 Hurricane Hunters fly close to the eye of a hurricane. These are special weather planes that fly into the storm in order to take measurements such as atmospheric pressure. It is a dangerous job for the pilots, but the information they gather helps to predict the hurricane's path – and saves lives.

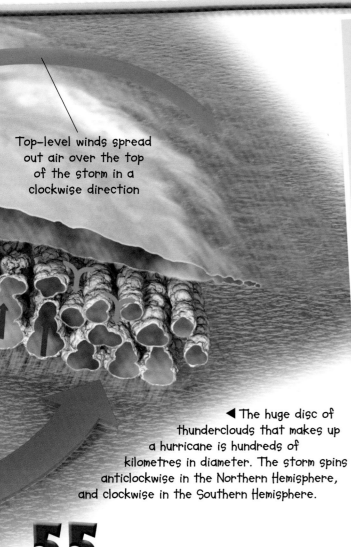

Top-level winds spread out air over the top of the storm in a clockwise direction

◀ The huge disc of thunderclouds that makes up a hurricane is hundreds of kilometres in diameter. The storm spins anticlockwise in the Northern Hemisphere, and clockwise in the Southern Hemisphere.

54 Hurricanes make the sea rise. As the storm races over the ocean, its strong winds push on the seawater in front of it. This causes seawater to pile up, sometimes more than 10 metres high, which hits the shore as a storm surge. In 1961, the storm surge following Hurricane Hattie washed away Belize City in South America.

▼ Massive waves crash onto shore in Rhode Island, USA, during Superstorm Sandy in October 2012. Sandy began as a hurricane, but was downgraded to a storm.

55 Hurricanes have names. One of the worst hurricanes was Hurricane Katrina, which battered the US coast from Florida to Texas in August 2005. The National Weather Service in the USA officially began a naming system of hurricanes in 1954, which has continued to the present day.

▼ A typhoon prevented Genghis Khan's navy from invading Japan.

56 Typhoons saved the Japanese from Genghis Khan. The 13th-century Mongol leader made two attempts to invade Japan – and both times, a terrible typhoon battered his fleet of ships and saved the Japanese!

Twisting tornadoes

57 Tornadoes spin at speeds of up to 480 kilometres an hour. These whirling columns of wind, also known as twisters, are some of Earth's most destructive storms. They form in strong thunderstorms, when the back part of the thundercloud starts spinning. The spinning air forms a funnel that reaches down towards the Earth. When it touches the ground, it becomes a tornado.

58 A tornado can be strong enough to lift a train! The spinning tornado whizzes along the ground like an enormous, high-speed vacuum cleaner, sucking up everything in its path. It rips the roofs off houses, and even tosses buildings into the air. In the 1930s, a twister in Minnesota, USA, threw a train carriage full of people over 8 metres into the air!

▶ A tornado can cause great damage to anything in its path.

I DON'T BELIEVE IT!

Loch Ness in Scotland is famous for sightings of a monster nicknamed Nessie. Perhaps people who have seen Nessie were really seeing a waterspout.

USA
Minneapolis
Sioux Falls
Chicago
Denver
Kansas City
St Louis
Wichita
Amarillo
Oklahoma City
Dallas
Houston
New Orleans
MEXICO

59 Tornado Alley is a twister hotspot in the American Midwest. This is where hot air travelling north from the Gulf of Mexico meets cold polar winds travelling south, and creates huge thunderclouds. Of course, tornadoes can happen anywhere in the world when the conditions are right.

60 A pillar of whirling water can rise out of a lake or the sea. Waterspouts are spiralling columns of water that can be sucked up by a tornado as it forms over a lake or the sea. They tend to spin more slowly than tornadoes because water is much heavier than air.

◄ Waterspouts can suck up fish from a lake!

61 Dust devils are similar to tornadoes, and form in deserts and other dry dusty areas. They shift tonnes of sand and can cause terrible damage – stripping the paintwork from a car in seconds.

◄ A desert dust devil in Amboseli National Park, Kenya.

Sky lights

62 Rainbows are made up of seven colours. They are caused by sunlight passing through raindrops. The water acts like a glass prism, splitting the light. White light is made up of seven colours – red, orange, yellow, green, blue, indigo and violet – so these are the colours, from top to bottom, that make up the rainbow.

◀ Rainbows are often seen after rain has stopped.

63 It is not just angels that wear halos! When you look at the Sun or Moon through clouds containing tiny ice crystals, they seem to be surrounded by a glowing ring of light called a halo.

64 Two rainbows can appear at once. This is caused by the light being reflected twice inside a raindrop. The top rainbow is a reflection of the bottom one, so its colours appear the opposite way round, with the violet band at the top and red at the bottom.

65 Some rainbows appear at night. They happen when falling raindrops split moonlight, rather than sunlight. This sort of rainbow is called a moonbow. They are very rare, and can only be seen in a few places in the world.

◀ A halo around the Sun or Moon can be a sign that a storm is coming.

REMEMBER IT!

The first letter of every word of this sentence gives the first letter of each colour of the rainbow – as it appears in the sky:
Richard Of York Gave Battle In Vain

Red Orange Yellow Green Blue Indigo Violet

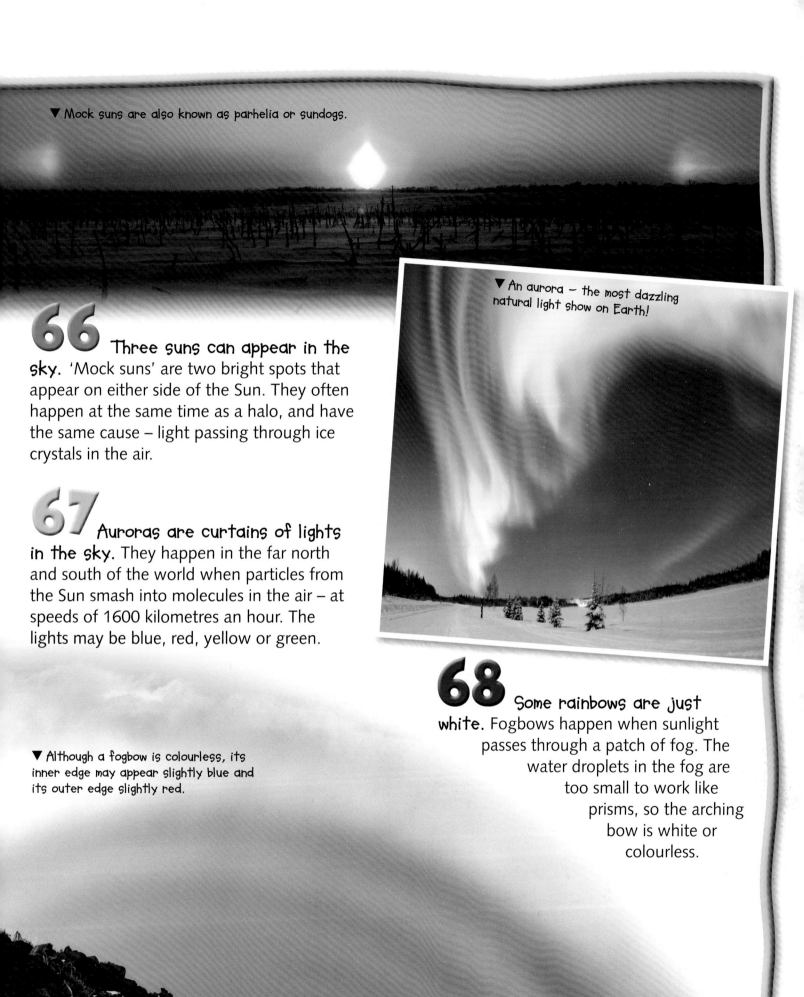

▼ Mock suns are also known as parhelia or sundogs.

▼ An aurora – the most dazzling natural light show on Earth!

66 **Three suns can appear in the sky.** 'Mock suns' are two bright spots that appear on either side of the Sun. They often happen at the same time as a halo, and have the same cause – light passing through ice crystals in the air.

67 **Auroras are curtains of lights in the sky.** They happen in the far north and south of the world when particles from the Sun smash into molecules in the air – at speeds of 1600 kilometres an hour. The lights may be blue, red, yellow or green.

▼ Although a fogbow is colourless, its inner edge may appear slightly blue and its outer edge slightly red.

68 **Some rainbows are just white.** Fogbows happen when sunlight passes through a patch of fog. The water droplets in the fog are too small to work like prisms, so the arching bow is white or colourless.

Animal survival

69 Camels can go for two weeks without a drink. They are adapted to life in a hot, dry climate. Camels do not sweat until their body temperature hits 40°C, which helps them to save water. Their humps are fat stores, which are used for energy when food and water is scarce.

◄ Many desert creatures, such as this gecko, come out at night when it is cooler.

70 Lizards lose salt through their noses. Most animals get rid of excess salt in their urine, but lizards, such as iguanas and geckos, live in dry parts of the world. They need to lose as little water from their bodies as possible.

◄ Being able to withstand long periods without water means that camels can survive in the harsh desert environment.

71 Even toads can survive in the desert. The spadefoot toad copes with desert conditions by staying underground in a burrow for most of the year. It only comes to the surface after a shower of rain.

◄ Beneath its gleaming—white fur, the polar bear's skin is black to absorb heat from the Sun.

72 **Polar bears have black skin.** These bears have all sorts of special ways to survive the polar climate. Plenty of body fat and thick fur keeps them snug and warm, while their black skin soaks up as much warmth from the Sun as possible.

73 **Acorn woodpeckers store nuts for winter.** Animals in temperate climates have to be prepared if they are to survive the cold winter months. Acorn woodpeckers turn tree trunks into larders. During autumn, when acorns are ripe, the birds collect as many as they can, storing them in holes that they bore into a tree.

◄ Storing acorns for food helps this woodpecker survive the cold winter months.

Myths and legends

▲ The Egyptian sun god, Ra, was often shown with the head of a falcon.

74 People once thought the Sun was a god. The sun god was often considered to be the most important god of all, because he brought light and warmth and ripened crops. The ancient Egyptians built pyramids that pointed up to their sun god, Ra, while the Aztecs believed that their sun god, Huitzilpochtli, had even shown them where to build their capital city.

75 Hurricanes are named after a god. The Mayan people lived in Central America, the part of the world that is most affected by hurricanes. Their creator god was called Huracan.

▼ Viking myths tell how Thor was killed in a great battle by a giant serpent.

76 The Vikings thought a god brought thunder. Thor was the god of war and thunder, worshipped across what is now Scandinavia. The Vikings pictured Thor as a red-bearded giant. He carried a hammer that produced bolts of lightning. Our day, Thursday, is named in Thor's honour.

77

People once danced for rain. In hot places such as Africa, people developed dances in the hope that they would bring rain. These were performed by the village shaman (a person thought to have a strong connection to spirits), using wooden instruments such as bullroarers. Sometimes water was sprinkled on the ground. Rain dances are still performed in some countries today.

78

Totem poles honoured the Thunderbird. Certain tribes of Native American Indians built tall, painted totem poles, carved in the image of the Thunderbird. They wanted to keep the spirit happy, because they thought it brought rain to feed the plants.

▶ A Native American Indian totem pole depicting the spirit of the Thunderbird.

MAKE A BULLROARER

You will need:
wooden ruler   string

Ask an adult to drill a hole in one end of the ruler. Thread through the string, and knot it, to stop it slipping through the hole. In an open space, whirl the instrument above your head to create a wind noise!

◀ A Mexican rain-dancer in traditional Mayan costume.

Weather folklore

79 'Red sky at night is the sailor's delight'. This is one of the most famous pieces of weather lore and means that a glorious sunset is followed by a fine morning. It is based on the fact that if rain clouds are in the east at sunset, meaning the rain has already passed, they light up red. The saying is also known as 'shepherd's delight'.

▼ A beautiful sunset could help a sailor to predict the next day's weather.

80 Seaweed can tell us if rain is on the way. Long ago, people looked to nature for clues about the weather. One traditional way of forecasting was to hang up strands of seaweed. If the seaweed stayed slimy, the air was damp and rain was likely. If the seaweed shrivelled up, the weather would be dry.

81 'Clear moon, frost soon'. This old saying does have some truth in it. If there are few clouds in the sky, the view of the Moon will be clear – and there will also be no blanket of cloud to keep in the Earth's heat. That makes a frost more likely – during the colder months, at least.

▶ The Moon is clearly visible when there are few clouds in the night sky. Its light casts a silvery glow over the Earth.

◀ Early Chinese weather-watchers recorded their observations on pieces of tortoiseshell.

82 The earliest weather records are over 3000 years old. They were found on a piece of tortoiseshell and had been written by Chinese weather-watchers. The inscriptions describe when it rained or snowed and how windy it was.

▶ Groundhogs emerge from their underground homes in spring following their winter hibernation.

83 Groundhogs tell the weather when they wake. In parts of the USA, Groundhog Day is a huge celebration. On 2 February, people gather to see the groundhog come out of its burrow. If it is cloudy and the groundhog has a shadow, it means there are six more weeks of cold to come. There is no evidence that this is true, though.

Instruments and inventors

84 The Tower of Winds was built by Andronicus of Cyrrhus in Athens, Greece around 75 BC. It is the first known weather station. It had a wind vane on the roof and a water clock inside. Its eight sides were built to face the points of the compass: north, northeast, east, southeast, south, southwest, west and northwest.

▼ This is how the Tower of Winds looks today.

85 The first barometer was made by one of Galileo's students. Barometers measure air pressure. The first person to describe and make an instrument for measuring air pressure was an Italian called Evangelista Torricelli (1608–1647). He had studied under the great scientist Galileo. Torricelli made his barometer in 1643.

◀ Torricelli took a bowl of mercury and placed it under the open end of a glass tube, also filled with mercury. It was the pressure of air on the mercury in the bowl that stopped the mercury in the tube from falling.

86 Weather vanes have been used since around 50 BC. They are placed on the highest point of a building, and have four fixed pointers to show north, south, east and west. A shape on the top swivels freely, so when the wind blows it points in the direction that the wind is blowing from.

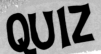

QUIZ

1. What was the Tower of Winds?
2. What did its sides face?
3. What do barometers measure?
4. Who made the first thermometer?

Answers:
1. A weather station 2. The points of the compass 3. Air pressure 4. Gabriel Daniel Fahrenheit

87 A weather house really can predict the weather. It is a type of hygrometer – an instrument that detects how much moisture is in the air. If there is lots, the rainy-day character comes out of the door!

◀ Weather houses have two figures. One comes out when the air is damp, and the other when the air is dry.

◀ Ships, cockerels and many other shapes are used to indicate wind direction on weather vanes.

88 Fahrenheit made the first thermometer in 1714. Thermometers are instruments that measure temperature. Gabriel Daniel Fahrenheit (1686–1736) invented the thermometer using a blob of mercury sealed in an airtight tube. The Fahrenheit scale for measuring heat was named after him. The Centigrade scale was introduced in 1742 by the Swedish scientist Anders Celsius (1701–1744).

▶ Anders Celsius came from a family of scientists and astronomers.

▲ This early thermometer shows both the Fahrenheit and the Celsius temperature scales.

What's the forecast?

89 Predicting the weather is called forecasting. Forecasters study the atmosphere and look at past weather patterns. They then use supercomputers to work out what the weather will be like over the next few days. But sometimes even forecasters get it wrong!

 A cold front is shown by a blue triangle

 A warm front is shown by a red semi-circle

 Black lines with red semi-circles and blue triangles show where a cold front meets a warm front

 White lines called isobars connect places of equal air pressure

 This symbol shows wind strength and direction. The circle shows how much cloud cover there is

 This symbol shows that the wind is very strong – look at the three lines on the tail

 This shows an area of calm, with some cloud cover

▲ Meteorologists call their weather maps synoptic charts. The symbols they use make up a common language for weather scientists all around the world.

▲ Meteorologists (weather scientists) use modern technology to accurately track and predict the weather.

WEATHER SYMBOLS

Learn how to represent the weather on your own synoptic charts. Here are some of the basic symbols to get you started. You may come across them in newspapers or while watching television. Can you guess what they mean?

90 Nations need to share weather data. By 1865, nearly 60 weather stations across Europe were swapping information. These early weather scientists, or meteorologists, realized that they needed to present their data using symbols that they could all understand. Today, meteorologists still plot their data on maps called synoptic charts. Lines called isobars link areas of the same air pressure and other symbols indicate temperature and wind.

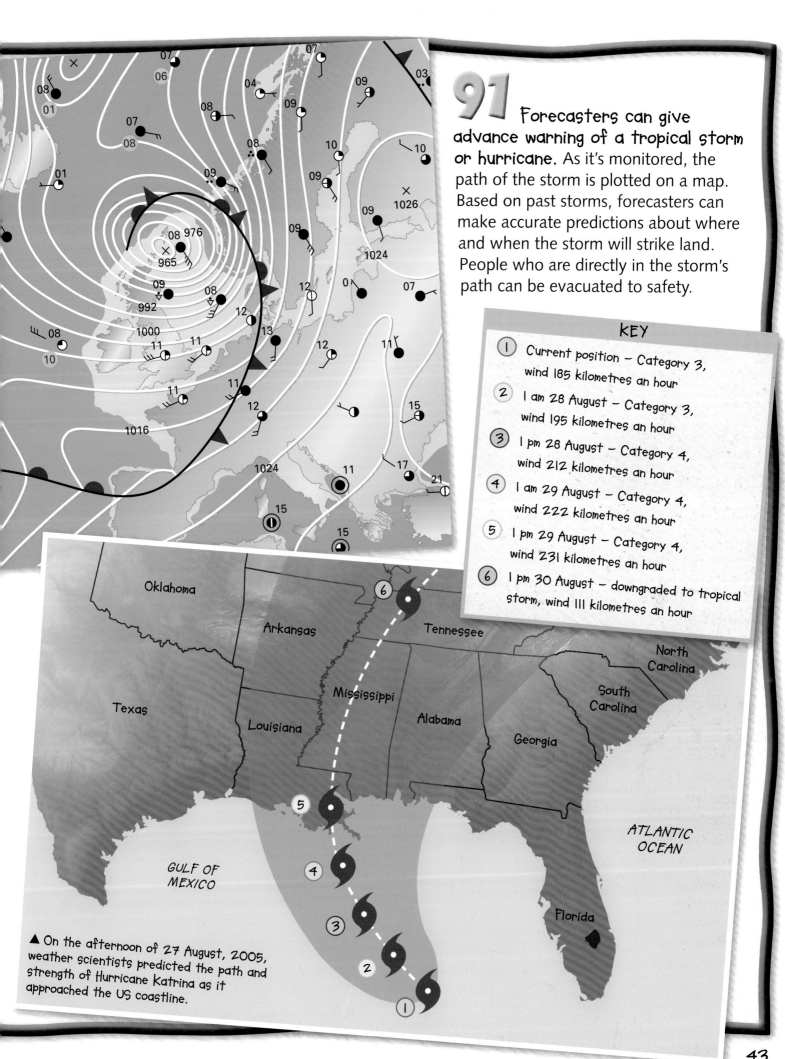

91 Forecasters can give advance warning of a tropical storm or hurricane. As it's monitored, the path of the storm is plotted on a map. Based on past storms, forecasters can make accurate predictions about where and when the storm will strike land. People who are directly in the storm's path can be evacuated to safety.

KEY

① Current position – Category 3, wind 185 kilometres an hour

② 1 am 28 August – Category 3, wind 195 kilometres an hour

③ 1 pm 28 August – Category 4, wind 212 kilometres an hour

④ 1 am 29 August – Category 4, wind 222 kilometres an hour

⑤ 1 pm 29 August – Category 4, wind 231 kilometres an hour

⑥ 1 pm 30 August – downgraded to tropical storm, wind 111 kilometres an hour

▲ On the afternoon of 27 August, 2005, weather scientists predicted the path and strength of Hurricane Katrina as it approached the US coastline.

43

Weather watch

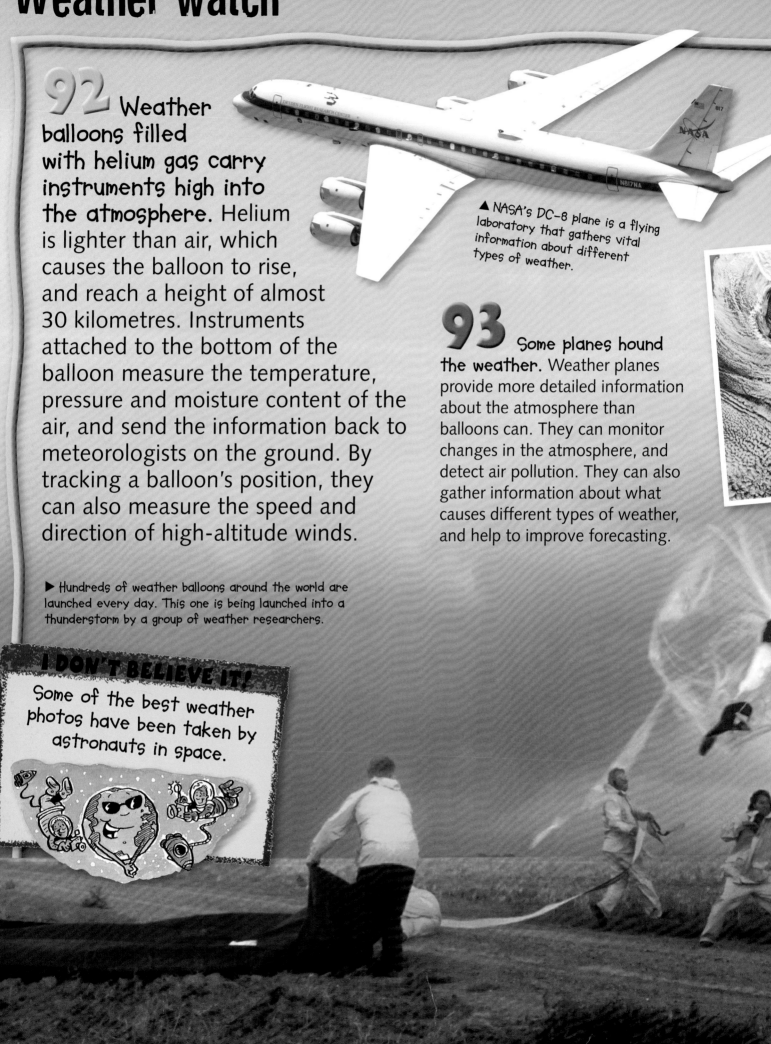

92 Weather balloons filled with helium gas carry instruments high into the atmosphere. Helium is lighter than air, which causes the balloon to rise, and reach a height of almost 30 kilometres. Instruments attached to the bottom of the balloon measure the temperature, pressure and moisture content of the air, and send the information back to meteorologists on the ground. By tracking a balloon's position, they can also measure the speed and direction of high-altitude winds.

▲ NASA's DC-8 plane is a flying laboratory that gathers vital information about different types of weather.

93 Some planes hound the weather. Weather planes provide more detailed information about the atmosphere than balloons can. They can monitor changes in the atmosphere, and detect air pollution. They can also gather information about what causes different types of weather, and help to improve forecasting.

▶ Hundreds of weather balloons around the world are launched every day. This one is being launched into a thunderstorm by a group of weather researchers.

I DON'T BELIEVE IT!
Some of the best weather photos have been taken by astronauts in space.

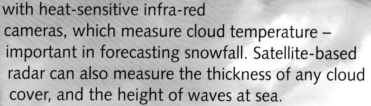

94 Weather satellites can provide a wide range of vital information. From such a long way above the Earth, their cameras can spot the distinctive spiralling cloud pattern of a tropical storm while it is still mid-ocean. This helps forecasters to issue warnings in good time. Satellites are also equipped with heat-sensitive infra-red cameras, which measure cloud temperature – important in forecasting snowfall. Satellite-based radar can also measure the thickness of any cloud cover, and the height of waves at sea.

▲ A weather satellite takes photographs of Earth's weather systems from space.

▲ A satellite photograph showing two spiral weather systems in the North Atlantic Ocean.

95 Ground-based weather radar that can detect rainfall and wind speed is used at airports. Knowledge of the exact weather conditions is critical for pilots during take-off and landing. Weather radar is also used to track the formation and path of tornadoes, and at sea, radar can give warning of icebergs.

▶ Weather information is collected from even the remotest parts of the globe. This weather monitoring station is inside the Arctic Circle.

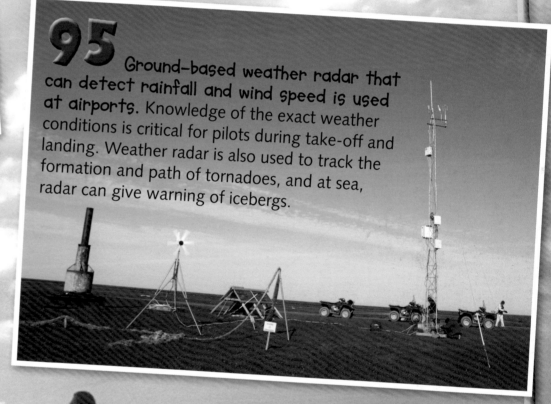

Changing climate

96 **Earth's climate is constantly changing.** There have been several major climate-change events during human history. The most recent was the Little Ice Age lasting from about 1550 to 1850, when average temperatures in some places were about one degree cooler than they are today.

Heat from the Sun

Trapped heat bounces back to Earth

Carbon dioxide layer traps heat

▲ Some gases in the atmosphere, such as carbon dioxide, create a 'greenhouse effect'. Without greenhouse gases, which trap heat, the Earth would be about 33° Celsius colder.

97 **Air temperatures are rising.** Scientists think the average global temperature may increase by around 1.5° Celsius this century. This may not sound like much, but the extra warmth will mean more storms, including hurricanes and tornadoes, and more droughts too.

▲ An iceberg breaks away from the end of the Hubbard glacier in Alaska. Climate change may be increasing the rate of iceberg production.

98
Tree-felling is affecting our weather. In areas of Southeast Asia and South America, rainforests are being cleared for farming. When the trees are burned, the fires release carbon dioxide – a greenhouse gas that helps to blanket the Earth and keep in the heat. High levels of carbon dioxide raise the temperature too much.

▶ Like all plants, rainforest trees take in carbon dioxide and give out oxygen. As rainforests are destroyed, the amount of carbon dioxide in the atmosphere increases.

99
Some sea creatures, such as the colourful corals that live mainly in shallow water, are very sensitive to temperature. As the atmosphere gradually warms up, so does the temperature of the surface water. This causes the coral animals, called polyps, to die, leaving behind their lifeless, stony skeletons.

◀ The death of corals through changes in water temperature is known as 'bleaching'.

QUIZ
1. When was the Little Ice Age?
2. Where do corals mainly live?
3. What gas is released when trees are burned?

Answers:
1. 1550 to 1850 2. In shallow water 3. Carbon dioxide

100
The long-term effects of climate change are uncertain. In the short-term it seems very likely that the climate will become more unstable, and that there will be an increase in the number and intensity of extreme weather events. Weather forecasting has always been important, but in the future it will become even more so as we adapt to Earth's changing climate.

Index

Entries in **bold** refer to main subject entries. Entries in *italics* refer to illustrations.